19'

SERVING IN THE ARMY

Alix Wood

PowerKiDS
press

New York

Published in 2014 by Rosen Publishing
29 East 21st Street, New York, NY 10010

Editor for Alix Wood Books: Eloise Macgregor
Designer: Alix Wood
Researcher: Kevin Wood
Military Consultant: Group Captain MF Baker MA RAF (Retd)
Educational Consultant: Amanda Baker BEd (Hons) PGCDL

Photo Credits: Cover, 4 top, 11 top © Shutterstock; 1, 4 bottom, 5, 6, 7, 8, 9, 10,
11 bottom and middle, 12, 13, 14, 15, 16, 17, 18, 19, 20, 21, 22, 23, 24, 25,
26, 27, 28, 29, 31 © Defenseimagery.mil; 19 bottom © Truman Library

Library of Congress Cataloging-in-Publication Data

APR 1 4 2014

Wood, Alix.
  Serving in the Army / by Alix Wood.
      pages cm — (Protecting our country)
  Includes index.
  ISBN 978-1-4777-1294-8 (library binding) — ISBN 978-1-4777-1394-5 (pbk.)
  — ISBN 978-1-4777-1395-2 (6-pack)
  1. United States. Army—Juvenile literature. I. Title.
  UA25.W625 2014
  355.00973—dc23

                                                    2013002104

Manufactured in the United States of America

CPSIA Compliance Information: Batch #S13PK3: For Further Information contact Rosen Publishing, New York, New York at 1-800-237-9932

Contents

What Does the Army Do?

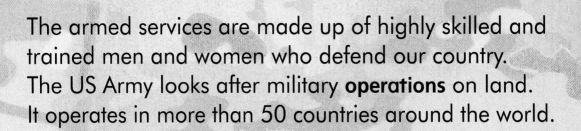

The armed services are made up of highly skilled and trained men and women who defend our country. The US Army looks after military **operations** on land. It operates in more than 50 countries around the world.

The modern army has its roots in the Continental Army, which was formed back in 1775. George Washington, the first US president, commanded the army during the American Revolution.

Reenactment of a battle from the American Revolution

The US Army is made up of several branches, from the infantry to military intelligence. They all have different roles to play in **combat** operations on land.

The salute is a gesture of respect and trust among soldiers. To salute, turn your head and eyes toward the person or flag you are saluting. Bring your right hand up, fingers together, until the tip of your forefinger touches the outer edge of your right eyebrow or the same area on the brim of your hat. Your upper arm should be **horizontal** to the ground. Then bring your hand straight back to your side.

FACT FILE

Army Ranks

Enlisted:

- Private
- Private First Class
- Corporal
- Sergeant
- Staff Sergeant
- Sergeant First Class
- First Sergeant
- Sergeant Major

Officers:

- 2nd. Lieutenant
- 1st. Lieutenant
- Captain
- Major
- Lieutenant Colonel
- Colonel
- Brigadier General
- Major General
- Lieutenant General
- General

Becoming a Soldier

When a new **recruit** joins the army, he or she goes through Basic Combat Training. This is a ten week course designed to turn young people into soldiers. New recruits learn the seven core army values, self-discipline, and how to work together as a team.

A recruit gets a haircut

Recruits build their confidence by competing in tough challenges.

During the first days of training, the recruits are given haircuts and issued uniforms. They also take a physical fitness test. Then they start to learn how to defend themselves in different types of combat situations. In the following weeks, they will learn how to handle different types of weapons. They will learn the basics, such as how to march.

FACT FILE

Seven Core Army Values

LOYALTY: To the Army, your unit, and other soldiers.
DUTY: Do what is asked of you.
RESPECT: Treat people as they should be treated.
SELFLESS SERVICE: Put the welfare of all before your own.
HONOR: Live up to Army values.
INTEGRITY: Do what's right, legally and morally.
PERSONAL COURAGE: Face fear, danger, or hardship.

Drill sergeants instruct and correct recruits in everything from firing weapons to the correct way to address a **superior**. They are also responsible for the recruits' safety.

Army Equipment

Having the correct equipment is essential. The army needs different supplies depending on where they are and what the **mission** requires. A woodland **camouflage** would not hide a soldier in the desert. A soldier's life can depend on his equipment.

The quartermaster is in charge of supplies. It's an important job. Quartermasters have to keep enough of everything from building supplies to boots in stock. When requests for supplies come in, they make sure everything gets to the right place.

These recruits are being issued their boots.

Body armor is made of bullet-proof material with ceramic plates inside. The fibers of the bullet-proof material are so tightly woven that they resist being torn apart. When the fibers stretch, they soak up the energy of the bullet.

Mount for night vision kit (see above)

Bullet-proof helmet

Bullet-proof vest

Pockets and clips for supplies

The army uses camouflage to help hide its troops from the enemy. Different camouflage patterns are used for different types of landscapes. The soldiers on the right are wearing woodland camouflage. The soldier above is wearing a desert pattern. Camouflage helps break up the soldier's outline and makes him or her harder to see.

Infantry Soldiers

The infantry is the main land combat force and the backbone of the US Army. It is responsible for defending our country against any threat by land, as well as capturing, destroying, and pushing back enemy ground forces.

The infantry needs to be able to enter enemy territory. These army rangers (below) are practicing carrying an injured soldier across open country. Walking out in the open is very dangerous for troops. There is no cover and they are easy targets for enemy fire. The infantry carry light weapons, such as rifles and pistols.

Infantry on sentry duty in Iraq

When troops practice what they would do in a war situation, it is called an "exercise."

To provide cover for troops out in the open, the infantry has specialists that can fire mortars or use small machine guns. This equipment is heavy to carry. Often the specialist carries the mortar barrel and others carry a mortar shell or two each. They leave the mortars at a drop site for the specialist to use. Cover fire disrupts the enemy and may even stop enemy fire.

Searching a building is very dangerous. An enemy can hide behind doorways. Soldiers use a technique called "slicing the pie" to scan the room beyond a doorway while keeping themselves hidden. See the diagram below. You move left while looking in the direction of the arrows. The pale area is the danger area.

Mortar

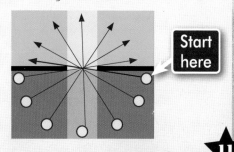

Start here

Snipers and Marksmen

The main difference between a marksman and a sniper is that a marksman is usually part of a team of soldiers. It's his job to take accurate long-range shots at targets. Snipers tend to work alone or with other snipers and sneak up on the enemy.

Snipers usually work in pairs. One shoots the sniper rifle and the other spots the target with the **scope**. When the sniper fires, the spotter works out where the bullet hit and directs the sniper to the target if he has missed it. The spotter carries a radio, an assault rifle, and a grenade launcher.

A sniper's rifle

A spotter's scope

Spotters can radio in the position of an enemy. Snipers often don't shoot at all. They just use their **stealth** tactics to find out where the enemy is.

Ghillie suits (right) are used by snipers when normal camouflage isn't good enough. They are designed to look like grasses and leaves. The suit moves in the wind like its surroundings. Snipers often add local leaves to blend in with their hiding place perfectly.

A sniper wearing a ghillie suit

While snipers are trained in **fieldcraft** and camouflage, these skills are not required for marksmen. A marksman is a normal soldier who has had extra marksmanship training. He moves with his unit and is equipped in the same way, apart from carrying a very accurate semi-automatic rifle.

This marksman is taking a position on high ground.

Armored Cavalry

The cavalry was originally the **mounted** force of the army. The armored cavalry began to replace the horse cavalry after World War I. The armored cavalry uses tanks and wheeled vehicles.

The Cougar is an armored fighting vehicle designed to protect soldiers against exploding mines and other weapons. Its V-shaped underside helps to direct explosions away from the vehicle. Air-conditioning helps keep heavily dressed troops from overheating. It can get very hot in a metal vehicle in the desert!

A Cougar during an explosives test

The Cougar above was hit by a large explosive device in Iraq. All on board survived and were back to work the next day!

The High Mobility Multipurpose Wheeled Vehicle, known as the Humvee, is a four-wheel drive military vehicle. It has a fully armored passenger area protected by hardened steel and bullet-resistant glass. It is one of the most common vehicles in the modern cavalry.

A Humvee can be fitted with a mounting unit for machine guns and grenade launchers.

Abrams Tank Crew

The M1 Abrams tank is armed and armored. It has a four-person crew, made up of a driver, a gunner, a loader, and a commander. Inside the tank is hot and noisy. It is hard to see out through the small windows.

The driver sits at the front under the main gun. To fit, he has to lean back in a bucket seat. He steers the tank using a motorcycle-style handlebar, with a handle grip throttle. The brake pedal is on the floor, as it is in a car. The driver navigates using three **periscopes**. At night he uses a night vision sensor.

The commander is in charge of the tank and communicates with other tank commanders. He uses periscopes to look out. The gunner fires the main gun. He pinpoints targets using a sight and a **laser** range-finder that measures the distance to the target. He also controls the front machine gun. The loader loads the main gun. The loader and commander may also operate the two machine guns mounted on top of the turret.

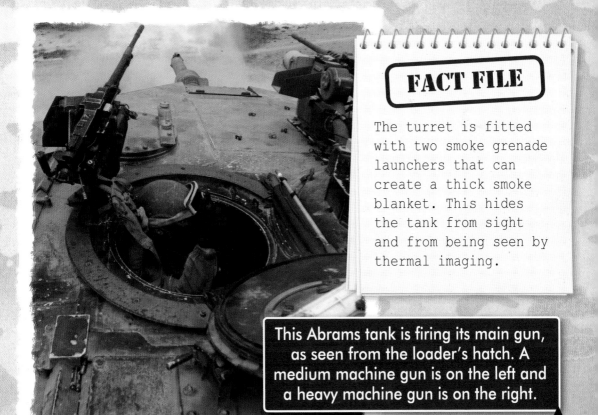

FACT FILE

The turret is fitted with two smoke grenade launchers that can create a thick smoke blanket. This hides the tank from sight and from being seen by thermal imaging.

This Abrams tank is firing its main gun, as seen from the loader's hatch. A medium machine gun is on the left and a heavy machine gun is on the right.

Field Artillery

Field artillery soldiers take on the enemy from miles away using cannon, rockets, and missiles. Some guns can be carried into position, but others are too large.

The M777 howitzer below is one of the main field artillery weapons. This large gun needs a crew of five to operate it. Although the M777 is a "light" artillery gun, it takes a 7-ton (6-t) truck to move it into position. The team must transport the gun, get it into position, load, aim, and fire. It can be quite noisy!

The team needs to work together to load and fire the gun.

Pod with rockets

The M270, above, fires missiles that can hit targets 190 miles (300 km) away! Each pod contains six standard rockets or one guided missile. The M270 above has one pod with six rockets loaded. It can also carry two pods, as shown in the picture on top left. The rockets don't travel as far as the missiles. The M270 can be used in "shoot-and-scoot" tactics. It fires its weapons quickly and then moves away to avoid being hit when the enemy fires back.

Army Rangers

As if the challenge of basic training wasn't enough, some soldiers go on to Ranger School, a 61-day combat leadership course. Not everyone who passes automatically becomes a US Army Ranger, but no one who has not been to Ranger School can become a US Army Ranger.

At Ranger School, soldiers are put through tough tests of strength and fearlessness. Ranger students train about 20 hours per day, eat very little, and get hardly any sleep. They must carry heavy weapons and equipment for over 200 miles (322 km) during the course. Only the toughest pass the test.

Here, a soldier crawls through the muddy "worm pit" at Ranger School.

This soldier is practicing his stream-crossing techniques.

FACT FILE

Ranger school tests include these tough fitness tests:
Push-ups: 49 (in 2 minutes)
Sit-ups: 59 (in 2 minutes)
Chin-ups: 6 (performed from a dead hang with no lower body movement)
5-mile(8-km)run In 40 minutes or less over rolling country.

Ranger School is hard. Soldiers spend hours walking fast with heavy packs, sleeping outside, and eating less than normal. Most students lose a lot of weight. The course teaches soldiers how to overcome challenges and prepares them for combat. If they pass, they can wear the well-deserved Ranger tab on their shoulders.

RANGER

If you pass, you have a chance to join the 75th Army Rangers. They are an elite special operations unit seen here parachuting out of a plane.

Air Assault!

101st Airborne Division, known as the "Screaming Eagles," is the army's helicopter-transported fighting force. It carries out air assaults, sending soldiers in to capture areas that are not fully secure by helicopter. These are dangerous missions.

Air assault forces are usually light infantry. The troops will be transported to the area by air. The equipment they need will be brought by air, too. This means that they usually only have small weapons and vehicles that can be carried by a helicopter. Equipment can be "sling-loaded" underneath the aircraft.

This team is sling-loading a gun onto a helicopter. It can be a dangerous operation. As the helicopter hovers just overhead, the soldiers must reach up to attach the load. It is so noisy that they can't hear. The wind from the rotors makes it hard to keep steady.

FACT FILE

Troops in an air assault may have to rappel out of a helicopter. To rappel means to quickly slide down a rope to the ground.

Rappel master

Step-by-Step:

1: Check the rope by pulling it.

2: Drop your bag and rope out. The rappel master makes sure the rope is touching the ground and free of tangles.

3: Sit with your legs outside the helicopter. Pivot round to face the rappel master with your feet shoulder-width apart, knees locked, and brake hand on the small of your back.

4: Bend your knees and push away. Let the rope pass through your hands. Move the brake hand out at an angle to slow yourself down. When on the ground, pull the rope clear.

The team is an easy target when it first hits the ground. It relies on fire support from the helicopters for protection.

Night Combat

Night combat takes place under cover of darkness. Combat at night usually benefits the attacker. Night makes it much easier to sneak up on a target, particularly one in the open that is hard to attack in the day.

Darkness affects a soldier's abilities in many ways. Soldiers focus more on what they can hear. Working in smaller units is best, as communication is easier. Training and planning are very important. Each soldier needs to keep contact with the other members of his unit. Clear, simple plans work best at night. It is easy to lose track of each other and the enemy.

The view through a thermal weapon sight

Soldiers have equipment that helps them work at night. Thermal imaging cameras show differences in temperature. Warm objects glow white and cool objects are darker. Warm-blooded humans are easily visible, day or night.

FACT FILE

Night vision devices use special tubes to collect any available light and boost it to make images. The green pictures here are typical of what you see through a night vision device. They are colored green because the human eye can tell more shades of green apart than other colors. They don't work well in fog or smoke.

Night combat is risky, but can be very successful. It can take the enemy completely by surprise. Often night combat will follow a day when soldiers have started to gain control in battle. It keeps the enemy from getting any rest.

Communications

Sending and receiving information is vital to the army. The Signals Corps is responsible for the army's communications systems. Years ago, signals were sent over long distances by waving flags or flashing lights. Now, the job is a lot more complex.

Soldiers use the latest technology to talk to each other. They can use a radio or send messages by satellite or computer. The enemy will want to listen in to their conversations, too. It is important that communications be secure.

Military satellite antennae

The army uses its own secure satellites in space, with large antennae on the ground. Some satellite systems act like regular mobile phone networks. The phones work in difficult areas like dense forests, too, because they use a low **frequency**.

Radio antenna

A soldier sets up mobile communications

The Signal Corps is the most technologically advanced part of the US Army. It has created or worked on new communication methods such as the telegraph, radar, FM radio, and satellites. In 1958, with the US Air Force's help, the Army Signal Corps launched the world's first communications satellite.

The Future

Robots are being developed to help the troops of the future. They can help **defuse** bombs, search buildings using cameras, or even help carry wounded troops to safety. Robots don't get sick, they don't need sleep, and they always follow orders.

The Battlefield Extraction-Assist Robot (BEAR) is being developed to carry wounded soldiers away from the battle area. It can carry heavy objects over long distances, and even go up stairs. The BEAR's hands are strong but gentle enough to pick up an egg without breaking it.

BEAR's teddy bear face gives friendly reassurance to an injured person.

Laser weapons are a possible weapon for the future, but at the moment they are pretty huge! This laser has to be transported on an eight-wheeled heavy-duty truck. The laser is very fast and accurate, though.

A high-energy laser "death ray"

The PackBot (top of the page) and the TALON (below) are already in day-to-day use. Between the two of them, they can be fitted with bomb disposal kits, **hazardous materials** detection kits, detectors that can sniff out explosives, or sniper-finder kits that use a sound direction finder to spot where gunshots came from. They can also carry day or night color cameras and listening devices.

Glossary

camouflage (KA-muh-flahj)
The hiding or disguising of something by covering it up or changing the way it looks.

combat (KOM-bat)
Active fighting in a war.

defuse (dih-FYOOZ)
To remove the fuse from an explosive device and make it safe.

fieldcraft (FEELD-kraft)
Ability and experience in living outdoors, especially in a wild area.

frequency (FREE-kwen-see)
The number of sound waves or waves of electromagnetic energy that pass a fixed point each second.

hazardous materials
(HA-zur-dus muh-TEER-ee-ulz)
Solids, liquids, or gases that can harm people, other living organisms, property, or the environment.

horizontal
(hor-ih-ZON-til)
Parallel to the horizon.

laser (LAY-zer)
A device that uses the natural vibrations of atoms or molecules to generate a narrow beam of light.

mission (MIH-shun)
A task or job given to the military to complete.

mounted (MOWNT-ed)
Using horses or vehicles.

30

operations
(AH-puh-ray-shunz)
Coordinated military actions
of a state in response to a
developing situation.

periscopes
(PER-uh-skohps)
Instruments containing lenses
and mirrors by which observers
can get views that would
otherwise be blocked.

recruit (rih-KROOT)
A new soldier.

scope (SKOHP)
An instrument for viewing.

stealth (STELTH)
Not attracting attention.

superior (soo-PEER-ee-ur)
Someone of higher rank
or importance.

WEBSITES

Due to the changing nature of Internet links,
PowerKids Press has developed an online list of
websites related to the subject of this book.
This site is updated regularly. Please use this
link to access the list:

www.powerkidslinks.com/poc/army/

Read More

Cooke, Tim. *US Army Special Forces*. Ultimate Special Forces. New York: PowerKids Press, 2012.

Goldish, Meish. *Army: Civilian to Soldier*. Becoming a Soldier. New York: Bearport Publishing, 2010.

Harasymiw, Mark A. *Army*. US Military Forces. New York: Gareth Stevens Publishing, 2011.

Index